THE POCKET GUIDE

to

CYBER SECURITY

Usha D & James H

Table of Contents

THE POCKET GUIDE TO CYBER SECURITY

About the Guide

This guide is aimed at an individual who is reasonably familiar with the basics of computing i.e. they know how to use a computer and the Internet well enough to make basic changes to settings on their computer. This guide is not intended as an in-depth technical guide. Instead, its aim is to provide some guidance for the average person who wants to improve upon their cyber security.

The information provided in this guide will allow the average computer user to assess their current cyber security situation and either directly improve their cyber security (i.e. configure their digital devices so that these are secure) or ask the right questions to an expert/forum/search engine if they are not confident about tackling the settings by themselves.

What is Cyber Security and Why Should I Care About It.

To many people, cyber security (aka information security or digital security) is a bit mysterious. It is something that many associate with Hollywood movies about spies and international espionage efforts by powerful and shadowy forces.

The reality is much more mundane. Cyber security is about protecting your digital information and data from accidental loss (i.e. dropping your laptop and smashing the hard drive) or theft/modification by everyday criminals (in most cases) not criminal masterminds.

It is also worth noting that your information won't necessarily be stolen by a 'hacker', because a 'hacker' (in the computer world) is someone who uses their skill with computers to overcome a problem. That problem may be attempting to get past or compromise a security system but this is also done by professionals with the aim of improving cyber security by finding out where security is weak and coming up with ways to strengthen it.

So, we won't use the term hacker here for our bad guy, we will use the term cyber crook or cyber thief. Note: the cyber security industry tends to use the term 'adversary', but we think cyber crook is more descriptive.

The aim of cyber security is to protect your digital information or data. Although the specific information or data that you would want to protect can vary, it could include:

- Letters to and from family and loved ones.

- Official documents that could be used to identify you i.e. your passport or birth certificate.

- It could be your credit card number and pin, or login details for your online bank accounts.

- It could be financial records or personal records that describe and prove your identity (or other people's identity if you have their information on your computer).

- It could be photos of you or your children.

In short, if it is information that you do not want anyone else to have, you should protect it.

Cyber security is perhaps less understood than home security (for example) because information doesn't feel quite as real to most people as home valuables. Everyone intuitively understands the need to lock up the house when you go somewhere; to protect the contents of the home from theft. But locking the digital door to your personal information is a bit more of a murky concept for most people. It is important to see your personal data and information as your property; it has value and it is worth protecting.

The people who would steal your digital property are not geniuses (although they are probably brighter than the average crook). They operate like a common thief, they look for a soft target or an easy opening to access your data and try to see what and how much they can get.

Poor cyber behaviour on your behalf is the digital equivalent of announcing to the world that you are going on a long overseas holiday. And how easy it is to gain access to your house; all crooks look for poor security and easy targets.

It is the aim of this guide to arm you with the information to make yourself a difficult target for cyber crooks, who often rely on ignorance about cyber security to steal your data. By the end of this guide, you will know enough to implement cyber security measures that will deter the average cyber crook, who will put you in the 'too-difficult basket' and move on to easier pickings.

We will now look at the ten main areas of focus in cyber security, these areas are used by businesses and governments when they are designing their cyber security strategy but they equally apply to the household. Let's take a look at the ten areas of focus for cyber security.

The Ten Areas of Focus for Cyber Security

We will discuss how you can improve your cyber security in each of these ten areas in greater detail in the coming chapters, but first let's get sense of what these ten areas are:

1. **Important Data**: the very first step you need to do to strengthen your cyber security is to determine what data or information is important for you to protect. There is not much point wasting time on protecting unimportant data.

2. **Password Security:** this involves knowing the best way to choose and use passwords so that cyber crooks can't easily guess or break through the log-in stage of your cyber defences.

3. **Malware protection:** malware (aka malicious software) is the prime method that bad guys use to spread viruses and worms (don't worry these terms will be defined later) that can damage your computer and/or your personal data. Malware is nasty and can really ruin your day and your

computer. It is essential to protect your digital devices with up-to-date malware protection.

4. **Phishing (Online Scams):** is nerd speak for fishing (as in fishing for a sucker), an online scam approach sent via emails, SMS etc. The aim of these scams is to present you with a convincing story and try get you to click on a link and provide data to a fake website (often designed to look legitimate). The data the crooks are after is usually your login credentials, financial information, or personal details. We will discuss how to detect a phishing attempt and avoid being landed by a cyber thief.

5. **Backup:** if you have ever lost a document that you were working on, you will understand the importance of backing up your data. It is the essential way to ensure that, if our data is compromised, all is not lost; and life can go on without the tears of frustration. Backing up seems like a simple concept but it is so often not done properly or done at all.

6. **Smartphone and Tablet Security:** in the age of smart phones and tablets, the way to protect these devices from attack or compromise is a little bit different and it's important to know how these can be secured.

7. **Our Cyber Behaviour:** how we behave in the cyber world is important because it is our actions that will ultimately result in how well our data is protected, you wouldn't walk through the bad part of town at night with a wallet full of cash; and it's similar in the cyber world. Cyber behaviour is also what we will teach our children who have access to

the cyber world a lot younger than their parents. Teaching kids safe and responsible cyber behaviour is just as important as teaching them safe behaviour in the real world.

8. **Cloud Security:** people are using the "Cloud" (which is really just a group of many servers owned and operated by a company) at various levels. One of the common ways this is used is to use applications/software and store data; instead of using laptop or local storage devices. People do this because it is cheap and can be accessed from anywhere and from many different devices (think of accessing your photos or documents from an iPad, smartphone, laptop from a central place such as iCloud or Dropbox). So that the information we place there and how the Cloud providers (such as Apple, Amazon) secure our information is an important consideration, and one we will discuss.

9. **Home Network Security:** for the slightly more advanced audience, this section discusses some basic home network security, which nine times out of ten consists of several devices (i.e. iPads, Laptops and Smart phones) connected to a Wi-Fi router, which has a cable connection to a wider Internet network. We will discuss the basics of home network security and provide some simple tips you can use to secure your home network.

10. **Physical Security:** this section provides an overview of what you should consider making sure your house is well protected from strangers getting access into your property to thieves attempting break in and steal valuables.

Focus 1: Important Data

Important Data: determining what data or information is important for you to protect and how it should be protected.

If you feel confused about what type of data/information you should classify as important then ask yourself; if I lost this information or something happened to change its accuracy or its currency, does this matter to me?

Here are some obvious examples of important data to help start your thinking:

- **Pictures and video:** Do you want your family photos to be lost or falling into the wrong hands? This used to be the first thing people wanted to save in a fire when photos were of the paper variety. Photos are memories and memories are considered highly valuable by most people.

- **Work/assignments:** What if you lost the novel you were working on, a big assignment or sensitive work information? Imagine how you would feel if it had been stolen and placed out there on the web?

- **List of contacts:** Imagine if you lost your collection of contact details, such as phone numbers; it would be a big task to get them all back, if it is at all even possible.

- **Financial information:** Being audited by the tax offices is no joke and it is seriously not funny if you lose all your tax receipts or previous tax returns. If you have other people's financial data, it is imperative you protect it.

- **Identity information:** Cyber crooks can take your personal details and if they have enough information, they can mimic your identity. Identity theft is quite sophisticated and hard for other organisations to detect early enough, especially if the identity thief is good at covering their tracks. Your best protection is to secure your identity information (such as your passport or driver's license) so that the cyber crook has too many gaps in your personal information to avoid suspicion when they try to impersonate you. This also applies to other people's identity if you have their personal information.

These are just a few main examples of important data to help you to get the picture. If you would be screaming to the sky 'why didn't I back this up or protect this' the moment it is gone, back it up (we will discuss how to do that in chapter 5). AND protect it.

Another useful habit to get into whenever you are saving a file or accessing information is to ask yourself the question, does this information matter to me? And if someone got hold of this information, could they make my life difficult, ruin my life or would it be no big deal?

Then ask yourself: how am I protecting this information? Or how is it being protected by the service that I'm choosing to use (i.e. Cloud storage)? If you are unsure about the answers to any of these questions, ask to find out and make sure you are happy with the answers.

How do we protect information?

Whether it is information in electronic or hardcopy form, if it matters to you, it should be carefully stored and protected; so that people (e.g. your kids messing around with your computer or a cyber crook) are unable to: get access to, modify or use your information in any manner (in more technical terms, this is called protecting the confidentiality, integrity and availability of the information).

Methods of protecting your information fall into these broad categories:

- **Protecting electronic information whilst it's in transit or transmission:** this is done using encryption (turning your information into an unreadable code) when it is sent from one digital device to another, where the unreadable code is then decoded only by the intended device with a decoding key; not a cyber crook stealing your data when it is half way between devices (technically known as a man-in-a-middle attack undertaken using some specific computer programs and tools).

    <u>Encryption over the Internet</u>
    A common example of this is making sure the website address (known as URL, e.g. www.something.com) you are accessing starts with https:\\ (the s stands for secure) instead of the old http:\\. HTTPS means that your data is securely passing between the web browser (such as Google or Yahoo, technically known

as the client software on your computer) via which you are accessing the website to the location where the website is hosted (technically known as a web server). It is worthwhile to always ensure that the websites you are accessing always start with https:\\. Technically, this is explained as data transmitted via the Internet being encrypted using a secure protocol called Secure Socket Layer (SSL).

Encryption of files/folders

Another example is to encrypt files or folders that you want to email securely using software such as Winzip (with encryption enabled) or 7Zip. These allow you to set a password that must be entered before data and files can be unzipped. This will prevent any files that might be stolen in transit from being viewed and used by a cyber crook.

Encryption of Network

A more advanced example is an encrypted Virtual Private Network (VPN). People use this quite a lot when working remotely and connect to their office network. Sometimes, VPNs are also used by people at home for a more private and secure Internet connection. Essentially, VPN is an encrypted tunnel between your computer and another computer or server via which your data can pass. The type of tunnels and type of encryption used can vary. For example, it can be a point-to-point connection over the Internet (in these scenarios, the secure protocol for encryption protection would be SSL) or site to site from one location to another (in these scenarios, the security protocol in use is IPSec (Internet Protocol Security).

Note: encryption of devices is discussed below.

A more in-depth explanation to the above would be to also discuss the encryption keys and algorithms used within the protocols such as SSL/IPSec discussed above. Basically, the method of encryption can be symmetric (using the same algorithm keys to encrypt and decrypt) and key types (public and private keys). The algorithms used within these keys also add another layer of complexity because some algorithms have been successfully broken whilst others have not. Just know that there are varying degrees of strength to encryption that can provide different levels of security.

- **Protect the electronic information whilst it's stored (all electronic data is stored on a database, hard drive, USB, laptop)**: this is done via controlled access i.e. requiring username, password(s), and multi-factor authentication for access to stored data (e.g. your bank account). Multi-factor authentication is just a fancy way of saying a security check other than your username and password. It could be a code sent to your mobile phone when you want to complete a bank transaction that you must enter, it could also be your fingerprints or a SecurID authentication number on a token (usually a key tag or key ring) device that you have. Technically, this is referred to as something you know (your password), something you have (e.g. mobile phone or token key ring), something you are (e.g. fingerprint).

Data can be stored off-line, in which case it is out of reach of a cyber crook (but not an old style thief) or online where it is vulnerable to cyber crooks. If you are really concerned about cyber theft, store your important data off-line. That way, it is no longer vulnerable to cyber theft via the Internet.

Data can also be encrypted on your laptop or device (mobile phone, USB stick) by using encryption software (there are a number of providers of encryption software and new ones all the time). That way even if your laptop or device were to be stolen or remotely accessed in some way, your important data would be useless to a thief, either of the cyber or old-style variety.

- **Physically secure portable data storage devices and hardcopy information so it can't be accessed**: this simply means that for important information on a USB stick or piece of paper to be truly secure, it must be protected by physical security i.e. being locked in a lockable filing cabinet, safe or other secure storage place. This is also particularly important when you are travelling and carrying these devices with you (i.e. to an overseas conference/holiday), which is a time where you are more vulnerable to theft.

There is also a way to check if someone has attempted to illegally log on to your system and access your important data. The way you do this is to check your operating system's log files e.g. event viewer in Windows (press your Windows key and the "R" key together and type 'eventvwr.msc' into the text field to access the event viewer). Your computer will keep a log file of all-important system events such as logon attempts with what happened and when. If logon attempts were made when you were not using your computer, then you may have found the 'fingerprints' of a cyber thief. If this has happened, immediately disconnect from the Internet and upgrade your digital door: change passwords to all channels by which you can access your important data, such as Internet banking, email, etc.

The bottom line

- Know which data is most important to you, know where it is stored and how you pass it on.

- Ask yourself, if I lost this data would I beat myself up for being so stupid and not backing it up/protecting it from this day to doomsday. If the answer is yes, then the data is worth protecting.

- Remember, data can be protected when it is stored and when it is moving or in transit (i.e. when you email it). It is paramount to make sure that encryption is in place when it is in transit.

Focus 2: Password Security

The chapter aims to answer the question 'what is the best way to choose and use passwords so that the information that you are trying to protect can't be accessed by someone who shouldn't have access to it'.

Most people feel overwhelmed with the ever-increasing list of passwords that they must maintain. Most of us can barely remember the name of someone we met thirty seconds ago, let alone trying to remember the password to our superfund or car insurance company. There are tricks, however, to assist us in creating strong passwords that are easy to remember which we will discuss in the next section.

Passwords are also most secure if they are changed regularly; this requires more work but will provide you the very strongest password security if your passwords are well chosen. There are also special 'master' programs/applications that will manage your passwords for you, which we will discuss later.

A good way to choose passwords

The longer, more complex, and random a password is, the more difficult it is to be guessed by a cyber crook.

To get through your password barrier, cyber crooks use a technique known as brute force, which simply uses a computer program to continually (and extremely rapidly) input passwords from a comprehensive list of common passwords or likely list of combinations of numbers/letters/characters used in passwords.

These lists used in brute forcing your password can contain billions of password combinations, so it is very difficult to think of one that is easy to remember but not on that list. There is, however, a technique that will allow you to beat brute force (or give you a high chance of doing so) and create a password that is very hard to break and reasonably easy to remember and it is as follows:

*A typical password people use is something like the name of their pet and then the year they were born i.e. **Fido1982**.*

This is a very weak password and will take seconds to break using a brute force program.

A much better password could more accurately be called a passphrase and goes something like this:

My first job was at pizza hut and I was paid $250 per week.

*Which you can turn into **'MfjwaphaIwp$250pw'** so you have taken the first letter of this pass phrase and turned it into a very strong and random seeming password but one that you are going to have a good chance of remembering.*
A password like this will be much harder for a cyber crook to get through even by using a brute force program.

You could also use:

My first car was a [model year] [car model] and it cost .... etc.

Use your imagination and use a phrase that has instant meaning to you but no one else.

Different levels of access using passwords

Note that levels of access are a function that is not available everywhere, it should be available on your laptop or say a website that you manage but is not available on email accounts like Gmail or Yahoo!

Passwords are linked to a unique username (usually your email address) to confirm your identity and (if correct) will provide you access to a given system. A user profile can be associated with differing levels of user access on a system sometimes called 'privileges'. That is, you can set-up your system so that people can use it i.e. friends and family but without them being able to do any damage to your data i.e. delete information. Two typical levels of access are user and admin (computer administrator).

Password managers

If you feel completely overwhelmed by the number of passwords you need to remember, there are special applications called password managers, which are software or services (although there are also free ones available) which will securely manage all of your passwords; they log all of your passwords behind an extremely secure login (which will be one very strong password that you must remember). Examples of password managers include:

- Password Safe.

- Password Manager(s) web browsers (e.g. Google Chrome, Internet Explorer).

- Password manager apps for iPad/iPhone (e.g. LastPass, DataVault, 1Password).

Note: if you forget the master password for your password management tool, it will prove to be extremely difficult to access all the other accounts that you have secured using this program.

The bottom line:

- Passwords must be long (over 12 characters); include numbers, symbols, and special characters (%#@%^ etc); must not be a dictionary word or combination of dictionary words.

- Passphrases make the best passwords.

- Users can have different levels of access where higher levels of access i.e. admin access have the potential to do more harm to your data and information.

- Change passwords regularly, at least every 30-60 days.

Focus 3: Malware Protection

Malware is a combination of the words malicious and software. It includes any software that is written with malicious intent and includes things like viruses, worms, trojan horses etc.

Note: malware is sometimes used interchangeably with 'virus' but malware is the broader category of malicious software. Malware is intended to harm the target computer user e.g. by extracting some valuable information such as login details or financial information. It's essential to protect your digital devices and systems with up-to-date malware protection.

What is malicious software and how does it work?

Malicious software is a piece of computer code that has been written by developers with malicious intent (i.e. black hat hackers – as we discussed there are many types of hackers). It is usually distributed in common file types attached to your emails, circulating on social media or direct you to websites where these files are downloaded (most of the time without your knowledge, technically this is called 'drive by downloads'). These file types have code that can be executed or run (meaning something can be changed on your computer). Usually, these file types end with the following extensions: .exe, .com, .jar, .msi, .bat, .scr, etc.

The intent or purpose of the malicious code can vary; different types of malware with different aims are called by different names, and a list of commonly seen malware is as follows:

- **A root kit:** a root kit is malware designed to give the cyber bad guy root (or administrative) access to your computer system (the highest form of access) once the bad guy has root access to your system, they can cause you much more harm.

- **Adware:** is malware in the form of misleading advertisements, pop ups and installed software that gathers information on a user's web behaviour, and is used to target them with ads to lure them to make a purchase (this is less harmful than other malware but still annoying).

- **Bot/Botnet**: are programs that attackers install on your computer allowing attackers to take control. The more machines are infected, a network of these are formed allowing the attacker to control and attack other systems.

- **Key loggers:** key loggers are malware designed to log all your keystrokes, usually with the aim of working out your username and passwords.

- **Ransomeware:** malicious programme that can encrypt important files on your computer (so that you cannot access them), lock you out of your computer or delete your data. The aim is to perform this type of malicious activity and withholding until a ransom (i.e. a payment in the form of money or crypto currency) is paid in return for decrypting/returning the files or unlocking the screen for access.

- **RAT:** Remote Access Trojan (RAT) allows a malicious actor to create a backdoor (or means of bypassing computer security and date encryption) into the user's computer allowing them to access the user's system without their knowledge.

- **Spyware:** spyware is software that was once accidentally installed on your computer, collects data and information about you, which sites you visit, who you talk to, etc.

- **Trojan horses:** a Trojan horse is (like in the Greek myth) designed to look like a legitimate program or software but once you click on it, it executes a malicious code that can harm your computer system. These programs can spy on you, steal data or get access to your computer.

- **Viruses:** are the most common form of malware, a virus is a malicious computer code that attaches itself to a file, program or document that supports macros, and copies itself to other software or programs. The virus will remain dormant until a built-in condition triggers it to start spreading through your computer system. Once triggered, a virus can damage your operating system (OS) by corrupting or deleting data, stealing information and changing data.

- **Worm:** a worm is malware that can replicate itself and spread through a computer network without needing a host program. It can spread by exploiting holes on computer system code or tricking users into opening the files and running the code so that it spreads.

Note: Malware can also have no monetary motive, it can simply be employed against users to cause them harm for the sake of causing harm. So, as you can see, the people who attack users via malware are no good at all and need to meet a very strong digital door (in the form of strong malware defence) to keep them out of your digital devices and out of your life.

Malware mostly propagates via fraudulent emails and installs in the background when the user clicks on website links or opens attachments (usually executable files e.g. .exe files that we mentioned before). However, there are other channels (or means of delivering malware). Some other examples of malware channels include USB memory sticks (provided for free, left in hotels as samples etc.), SMS sent to you with a cover story about why you should click on a malicious link, phone calls where an individual at the other end of the line directs you to a website to install a file; websites shared on social media platforms (such as Facebook) often use the pretence that it will protect you against malware.

Example of malicious spam email:

How do you know if you have malware on your computer? And what do you do if you have malware?

If you suspect there is malware on your machines, some signs, or symptoms to look out for are:

- Screen freeze.

- Messages demanding payment (in the form of money or crypto currency payment).

- Loss of files.

- Loss of operation or slow operations (i.e. you cannot visit the websites or download items like you usually do).

- Unusual behaviour of the machine compared to what you remember as the status quo (e.g. blue or blank screens).

- Computer crashes for no good reason.

- Slow operation of system.

- Error messages.

- Random pop ups or fake messages (ads encouraging a download or alerting you that there is something wrong with your computer).

- Run out of hard drive space and you have not saved or downloaded any large programs.

- Software such as your computer firewall/antivirus stopped working.

- Newly installed software - such as toolbars on your web browser software (e.g. Internet Explorer or Google Chrome) which you did not do.

If you have malware, you can use your anti-virus removal software, or a special program called a virus removal tool to get rid of the malware. If worst comes to the worst, you may need to format your hard drive (which wipes all information from it including all malware).

How can you protect systems against malware?

The best method of protecting against malware is to have an anti-malware program implemented on the devices which you use (in the past this was usually called anti-virus). These programs should be kept up to date and used to scan your systems regularly. Anti-malware programs have lists of signatures, which are pieces of code that can be used to identify the presence of malware. For example, if the anti-malware program scans your system's files and finds a signature match, it will have detected malware and will automatically quarantine the suspect file, stopping the malware from causing more harm to your system.

Various anti-malware solutions are available on the market at a cost. Open source or free ones could result in installation of additional malware on your system, so it is best to purchase industry recognised protective software.

Once purchased, regularly update your anti-malware program to ensure it is up-to-date (most of the time this will happen automatically) with the latest list of malware signatures downloaded to your laptop, to fight the most recent malware circulating the Internet.

There are instances where malware infiltrates systems before anti-malware code is developed and updated on people's systems (exploiting what are known as zero-day vulnerabilities which have no anti-malware program defence). The defence against this malware (which might get past your anti-malware program) is to ALWAYS be wary of what you install on your machine. Specialised software (known as Advanced Threat Protection) does exist to deal with zero-day malware code but is usually only available to large organisations not regular computer users due to its high cost.

In addition to having an anti-malware program installed on your computer it is advisable to remove all the software programs from your computer that you do not use on a regular basis. This is because all software programs will have some weaknesses in the code (technically known as vulnerabilities) which the crooks can develop malware to exploit.

Always keep your operating system (i.e. Windows, macOS), software/applications (i.e. Adobe), web browsers (i.e. Internet Explorer, Google Chrome, Internet Edge, Mozilla Firefox) and any plugins (such as Java) up to date with the latest versions. The companies that own this software are always findings holes or vulnerabilities in their programs, and they regularly release updates (technically called patches). So, if you keep the latest versions updated on your computer you will have the best available defence against malware exploiting your software.

Another trick you can use to protect yourself from malware is to enable "click-to-play plugins", this is a setting in web browsers that prompts you before your web browser runs any programs (such as Flash) in the background when you visit different websites. If you do not enable this setting these programs run automatically, and a lot of the time and this feature can be exploited by cyber crooks to automatically download malware on your computer when you visit certain sites.

If in doubt leave it out (or do not click on that link!!!).

How bad can a malware infection become?

Malware infection could completely wipe all files or information from an infected computer. It could also completely ruin the operation of a machine that you need day-to-day requiring you to reinstall your operating system (which will also delete all your data) or even cause you to have to replace your computer. And the impact of the malware can propagate to other computers that are connected to you (i.e. who you have as contacts via email, SMS or social media) the malware can also infect devices which are connected to the infected machine in your home network, such as other laptops, printers, television etc.

The bottom line:

- Install anti-virus or anti-malware software, keep it up to date and scan your computer regularly.

- Install or activate a firewall on laptop (a more sophisticated and advanced solution is called endpoint security protection which consists of anti-virus software, a firewall and monitoring for suspicious activities in one product.)

- Be aware of the programs which you are downloading and installing on your computer. If in doubt leave it out.

- Only use the programmes that you need on your computer and keep the ones which you use up to date.

Focus 4: Phishing
(Online Scams)

There are numerous types of online scams being thought up by cyber crooks every day. It is important to be able to detect what we are presented with (via text, email or other means) and recognise that it is a scam intending to take advantage of our trust, push us to react and cause us harm.

Phishing (aka fishing for a sucker) is a very common type of online scam, when you are fooled by attacker(s) pretending to be a trusted source, into handing over your information, such as account login credentials and/or credit card information.

In this section, we will discuss how to detect when you are being targeted by a phishing scam and what to do if you are caught by a cyber crook using a phishing attack.

What is phishing? What are the different types of phishing attacks?

Phishing is a scam where you are contacted (via email, SMS, mobile) by cyber crook(s) posing as someone else (the technical term for this is social engineering); usually as someone from a trustworthy institution (i.e. hospital, bank or well-known software company) or institution with legal authority (i.e. tax office or police etc). The cyber crook (or gang of crooks) usually wants your credentials which they intend to use to access something of value e.g. your online bank account. They may also want to steal some information that is important to you that you might pay the cyber crook to have returned, such as embarrassing photos or information that you wouldn't want to circulate on the Internet.

There are a few different categories of phishing scam (defined below) but almost all of these scams try to trick you into accessing a website (which you believe is legitimate), when in fact the website is a fake (set-up to mimic a website that you access frequently). Once you enter your login details (username, password) the phishing site captures this information and sends this to the cyber crook; who will then use your captured logon details to access your real account and perform unauthorised or malicious activities (e.g. transfer your funds to their account or make fraudulent purchases). In some instances, the phishing scam approach will be to try convince you to download an attachment in an email, to have you install malware.

In the cyber security world, there are different types of phishing attacks. These can be divided into following categories:

1. **Email phishing:** generic emails sent out to a mass amount of people, playing the numbers game, in the hope of catching someone (having them click on a link and providing some details).

2. **Spear phishing:** this is a personalised and targeted scam that targets you in particular (tailored emails to your name). This is a much more dangerous type of scam as it is harder to detect.

3. **Whale phishing:** this is specifically targeting businesspeople, having them perform a large financial transaction.

4. **Voice phishing:** also known as vishing is when you answer a phone call or receive a voicemail directing you to perform a task, transaction or ring a number to pay a fine.

5. **SMS phishing:** SMS or text message is sent with a link encouraging you to click on it to download malware/trojan.

6. **Baiting:** promising the victim an item, such as a winning prize to lure them to respond to the email and provide the information.

Note: Phishing attacks may also involve getting you to call a number which diverts to a fraudulent call centre. Be wary of any 'call centre personnel' asking for money or Bitcoin (a sure sign of a scam) or unusual details like your bank account logon or credit card details. Or requesting you to pay a bill for a service that you didn't ask for i.e. they might offer to upgrade your anti-virus software to something more expensive or claim you have thousands of viruses on your device that only they can remove. Don't be afraid to challenge any 'call centre operator' that is pushy or threatening, if all else fails simply hang up on them and report them to your local scam watch authority, for example in Australia this is https://www.scamwatch.gov.au.

How can I look out and protect myself against phishing scams?

It is advisable to always check and question any email or SMS which requires you to click on a link or install a file. Here are some tips to help you separate a scam from a legitimate request to click on a link or a file:

- Check the sender's name and email address. Is it someone that you know or just a general address with a masked name that appears like someone that you know? If you don't know the person or there is something not quite right about the address, don't open the email or click on any links.

- Use multi-factor authentication for important accounts: Multi-factor authentication is where you use something you know (e.g. your password), something that you have (e.g. your phone) and/ or something that you are (e.g. your fingerprint or signature) to gain access to a system. For example, two factor security is where, in addition to your username and password, your bank sends a code to your mobile for you to complete a transaction. That way even if you are a victim of a phishing attack and the cyber crook has your username and password, they won't be able to transfer money out of your account.

- Does the link that you are meant to click on look fishy with a questionable website name and hyperlink (e.g. www.somethingstrange.com), if it does, do not click on the link. Also, the way the link appears, and the actual link can be different. Hover your mouse over the link before you click on it to see if www.thebank.com (for example) is also the embedded link name (the text that shows up when you hover over links for a second or two), it might show up as something completely different alerting you that something is up.

• Does the content of the email or SMS read well? Or does it read like someone with poor English has written it (note: cyber crooks can buy kits to set up malicious websites and these are often not well structured, with badly designed logos, images etc.) if something is off, delete the email, preferably without reading it.

• Is the email sent from your own email address (known as spoofing)? You should NEVER receive an unexpected email from your own email address.

• Be suspicious of coercive or threatening language: Does the email sound threatening? Is it trying to pressure you to urgently go a website or hand over money? If it does, don't be intimidated, threats and coercion are not the tactics of a legitimate business or organisation, report the email to Scamwatch (https://www.scamwatch.gov.au) and delete it.

• Be suspicious of something that sounds too good to be true: Is a Nigerian prince likely to contact you about a great investment if you only send him your bank logon details? Are you likely to have won money when you can't remember entering the lottery a suspect email is talking about? Is that person on the other end claiming to be your boyfriend/girlfriend actually going to fly over and see you when you provide them with the credit card details to book their flight? If you receive any email urging you to go to a website to claim a financial reward, chances are it is a phishing email. Don't be the next sucker to fall for this type of bait, report the email to Scamwatch and delete it.

What do I do if I am a victim of a phishing attack?

If you feel you have been a victim of a phishing attack, turn off your digital device and switch off your Internet router so that any malicious activity will cease. If your compromised device is inactive, crooks with potential access to your system or accounts cannot monitor what is happening.

Attempt to capture what happened in chronological order, keep each note to a paragraph and number the paragraphs. If you have provided your credit card/banking details at any point in this process, inform your bank.

Using another device, change your online passwords for any compromised accounts, such as your online banking, insurance, email account(s), and ensure that these passwords are changed.

Contact the legitimate company being impersonated by the phishing attacker and inform them of the phishing attack method, show them screen shots of the phishing email and fake website.

Try to use another device to make these changes as your device is most likely to be under the crook's watch.

Depending on the extent of the compromise your laptop may need a rebuild (i.e. the operating system Windows, MacOS etc. might need to be reinstalled). All passwords to critical accounts that may have had related information in the compromised system or account MUST be changed. And monitor these accounts for any suspicious behaviour.

Report the online scam to the national cyber defence or scam watch group. In Australian Cyber Security Center (ACSC) https://www.cyber.gov.au/report

or Scamwatch
https://www.scamwatch.gov.au/.

The bottom line

- Implement multi-factor security on your bank accounts and other important accounts where it is available.

- Trust your gut. If an email, text or phone call seems suspicious or a bit unusual (e.g. spelling mistakes, unrecognisable email address, asking you to click on links) do not click on any links in it and report it immediately. You can also delete the email or hang up the call.

- If you think the email or message could be from someone you know but you are not sure, call and check if they sent it before you open an attachment or click on the link. Remember, their email account could have been hacked.

- It is not rude or unreasonable to ask someone contacting you to verify that they are acting in good faith.

- Do not be bullied or intimidated into taking an action that might compromise your cyber security NO ONE should coerce you into action using threats and intimidation.

Focus 5: Data Backup

The ultimate defence against our data being damaged, lost or compromised in some way is to back it up using a secure backup method. That way if things go really wrong you can recover your data and go on with your life with the least amount of pain and annoyance.

There is one simple concept when it comes to backing up your information. Store it separate to where it is currently stored. If you could store it somewhere physically separate (i.e. at a trusted family member's house) that is even better.

So, some suggestions are:

- Store it on a separate hard drive, such as a USB memory stick or hard drive, or even a laptop that is separate, and keep this device somewhere secure so that it cannot be accessed by anyone. Keeping it disconnected from the Internet will mean that it is also less exposed to online malware attacks.

- Ensure that the device you are using as backup isn't permanently connected to the device that you use regularly, so that if that is impacted by a virus, it doesn't spread to this drive.

- You need to consider what would happen in the case of a fire or your house being ransacked, if your backup and laptop (for example) are in the same house chances are you could lose both. Ideally you would store your backup in a secure location separate to where your primary data (i.e. laptop) is stored i.e. in a safety deposit box or trusted relative's home. Another idea is to store your backup in a hidden fireproof safe at your home.

Finally, another option is to use the data storage offered from a Cloud service provider. This could be a small amount of storage provided for free or a larger amount provided at a small cost. The Cloud has many advantages including automatic backup and the ability to access your data from anywhere; we will discuss Cloud security in more detail later.

A note on back-up devices

Not all back devices are equal. They have different expected lifespans (and durability) after which your data could be lost or corrupted. Services exist to recover data from a non-functional hard drive, and you can expect to pay around $1000 for a professional to attempt this but there are no guarantees that they will be able to recover all or any of your data.

All storage devices are, to some degree, affected by the ambient environment, that is, they may degrade faster if exposed to heat, cold, moisture or vibration. Storage devices last longest if these are stored in a cool (below 25° C) but not cold, dark and dry (low humidity) environment.

Here are a list of common storage devices and their robustness when it comes to storing data.

Device	Claimed lifespan	Possible lifespan with optimal conditions	Weaknesses
CD and DVD	5 years	25 years	Temperature, scratching.
Blue Ray	10 years	25 years	Temperature scratching.
M-Disc (special long-life storage disc)	1000 years	1000 years	Needs M-disc capable burner/reader.
HDD (typical hard drive)	5 years	10 years	Being dropped, repeated use, water.
Solid state drives (including flash drives)	10 years	If not used much possibly much longer	Heat, repeated use.

Table 1: Common Storage Devices Lifespan

As you can see, there are many different options for storage. You will need to decide which device is right for your data. You may have different data on different devices i.e. your photos you might want on a super robust M-Disc whereas your past financial records might be ok on a safely stored flash drive.

There should also be an option to encrypt USB and hard drives. This software should be provided with the devices which you purchase. If the information stored on these are worth encrypting (i.e. if the devices are stolen by someone, you want to prevent them from accessing your information).

The bottom line

- Store your back up data separately from your primary data at another property and preferably securely locked away. You can use offline and online options.

- The storage medium needs to be kept in a cool, dark, and dry place i.e. a safe or filing cabinet.

- Consider how long you need the data stored for; if you want to store you tax information, seven years is probably long enough. Family photos, however, you may want to think about long term storage i.e. an M-disc or the Cloud.

- Consider encrypting the data on your storage devices.

Focus 6: Smartphone and Tablet Security

We live in the age of smart phones and tablets, but do you realise that these devices need even greater security than your PC? (as these can be more easily stolen when you are on the go). Whilst operating systems like Windows on your PC might have a lot of holes or vulnerabilities that can be compromised, these tablets and smart phones run a lot of apps, which are created with code, and often 'bad code' that can lead to compromises. Most people do not consider the need to secure their smart phone or tablet from cyber crooks but they should. In this chapter we will discuss how smart phones and tablets are different to PCs and how to secure them.

How are smart phones and tablets different to computers?

The key difference between smart phones tablets, and the PC of course, is that these devices are much more mobile which affects how you secure them. Whether you realise it or not, your front door or office door provides you with some degree of cyber security, in that your PC (and thus your data) is less likely to be stolen from you (or lost or accidentally damaged) than your phone or tablet.

It is also worth noting that smart phones and tablets provide you with a means of distraction (through the many entertaining things they offer), crooks look for distracted targets. If you are walking down a dark alley engrossed in a message exchange with a friend you are the perfect target for a grab and run attack; before you are even aware of what has happened your phone/tablet and precious data will be running away from you in the hands of a thief.

What is available to protect these devices and how should we protect them?

Given the risks to your phone or tablet including loss, physical theft as well as cyber theft you should take care to secure them with these simple tips:

- **If you are walking alone be aware of your surroundings:** there is no need for paranoia but a healthy level of attention to what is going on around you makes you are hard target for a grab and run attempt on your phone or other mobile device.

- **Switch on password protection (screen protection):** this stops a cyber thief having easy access to data on your stolen phone or tablet.

- **Keep your devices up-to-date:** making sure your devices are up-to-date with the latest operating system (OS) version will insure you have the latest security patches installed; this will close up vulnerabilities in your device that could be exploited by a cyber-crook.

- **Keep your apps up-to-date:** as with your OS, old versions of apps loaded on your device open up vulnerabilities in your cyber defence, if you download the latest version of your apps many of these vulnerabilities will be eliminated or 'patched'. Only download and use the most essential applications; preferably from reputable application creators. The more applications you install, the more vulnerable your device will be to being hacked. Especially if these applications permit backend connectivity by someone into your system; a lot of the time these applications allow backend connectivity or share the same username and password to access it (e.g. using Facebook username/password to access other application).

- **Configure your devices so that they can be remotely tracked, locked or wiped:** you can do this yourself if you know what you are doing or you can use mobile device management software such as 'Jamf now' or 'find my phone'. This means if your device is lost or stolen, you can track it or lock cyber crooks out of your data so at least they won't be able to access it.

- **Do not connect to unknown or public wireless networks:** an unknown or 'free' wireless network that you connect to may be controlled by a cyber crook, which they can use to obtain your login details or access something you are working on while connected. The simplest way to avoid this is to not connect to any networks you don't control by using your 3G/4G/5G mobile data network (and tethering Internet hot spot to access that Internet service) instead of a free wireless network. Or if you have to connect to an unknown wireless network, do not access sensitive websites, such as your Internet banking, and ensure you have a personal VPN active.

What should we do if these devices become compromised?

If your device is lost or compromised, activate your mobile data security options to track and lock your mobile device and if all else fails, remotely wipe your data. You could also notify the police and register your device if you wanted assistance with finding your device or can be notified if an honest person hands it into lost and found at the police station.

The bottom line

- Switch on screen access protection and keep your apps and OS up to date for your devices.

- Use free mobile device management software to give you the option of remotely tracking, locking, or wiping data on your devices.

- Do not connect to unfamiliar or free wireless networks without a personal VPN. It is best not to use these at all, and instead utilise your mobile data to use the Internet.

- Be aware of your physical surroundings when using your phone or tablet so that you don't become a victim of a snatch and run theft. Don't be buried in your phone while walking alone at night for example.

Focus 7: Our Cyber Behaviour

How we behave in the cyber world is important because it is our actions that will ultimately result in how well we protect our data. Our cyber behaviour will also influence how our children behave online and they are online a lot younger than the adult of 2019; while many have had time to grow up and be aware of the extent to which we should trust strangers, before being introduced to the Internet.

As well as being bad for your character, bad or irresponsible cyber behaviour also exposes you to a higher risk of encountering a cyber crook, who will often use illegal temptations (i.e. gambling, pornography etc.) to snare their next victim.

Awareness of good cyber behaviour

When we enter the cyber world i.e. the world of the Internet, we need to keep the following in mind:

- Would I undertake this activity in person (i.e. not on the Internet but in the physical world)?

- Is what I am doing illegal?

- Is what I am doing ethical?

- Is what I am doing going to result in someone being hurt, shamed, bullied or abused?

Awareness of bad cyber behaviour

- Sometimes people are tempted to treat the Internet as a place with no consequences. In the real world they might be more introspective about how they behave, but online they might not feel the same behavioural restrictions apply. However, it is worth getting into the habit of acting online in a way that is consistent with how you act off-line.

- There are three distinct parts of the Internet 'the clearweb', 'the deepweb' and the 'darkweb'. The clearweb is anything accessible using a common search engine (i.e. Google or Yahoo) and is only 4% of the Internet.

- The 'deepweb' is all of the information that is not publicly and freely accessible using a common search engine; including things like information behind paywalls, data stored on Dropbox and webpages that are not indexed by a search engine (so you can't find them) and comprises 95% + of the Internet.

- The 'darkweb' is accessible only by using specialised software (i.e. Tor, a special type of browser). The 'darkweb' is the Internet's worst street in the worst neighbourhood; it is not exclusively used by criminals but it is a magnet for criminals and many illegal activities occur on it. Ask yourself would you go to the worst street in the worst neighbourhood in your city? If the answer is no, you probably should not access 'the darknet'.

- It might be helpful to continually reflect on your actions online and question if it is something that doesn't sit right with you. Reflect on your values and compare that to your behaviour online. For example, ask yourself, would you speak to people face-to-face the same way you speak to them online? If you cross the line and behave badly online, just as in real life, it is up to you to apologise and make amends. Remember, there is another human being on the other end of your screen.

- Likewise, with 'the darkweb', you are going to places in the cyber world that you would never go to off-line: illegal websites, gambling website etc. Be aware that in Australia, there are laws which regulate illegal online behaviour and penalties such as fines and jail time may apply for serious breaches of the law.

How do we teach our children good cyber behaviour?

Talk with your children about what is the right way to behave online and then set a good example for them to follow. Be part of their cyber world and pay attention to what they do online from the beginning. Don't let your children disappear for hours on end behind a locked door with their computer, for example. Take an interest in what they are doing online (whether it be gaming, social networks, Instagram, and even try to participate in it) and learn with them from a young age (this will allow you to stay one step ahead of them and protect them from any harm). Don't just discipline your children's online behaviour without explaining why you are doing it, if you restrict their online behaviour explain why you are doing it (and have a good reason).

Ultimately the best way you can teach children good cyber behaviour is if you are (reasonably) knowledgeable about the cyber world and model good cyber behaviour for them, children learn by example and aligning what you say with what you do builds trust.

Here are some suggestions to keep your children safe on-line:

1. Put your computer in a common area of the house.

2. Do NOT let them chat to strangers on chat applications. Ask them to tell you if they are contacted by someone they don't know.

3. Educate your kids that everything is not how it appears on the Internet, the nice person they are chatting with who seems to be about their age might actually be an adult who intends to do them harm, caution (but not paranoia) is required online.

4. Do NOT let children use all their personal details to register for games, chat applications, social network websites etc. Tell them why this is not a good idea as they don't know who will now have access to them.

5. Block in-app purchases and disable one click payment options on all devices.

6. Discuss the fact that you will review the browser history of your children to make sure they are safe online. If they do not have a browser history, ask them if they are deleting it?

7. Network with other parents to discuss any problem websites or content.

8. Educate your children about privacy settings on apps and things like Facebook.

9. Educate your children about why they should be careful about what they post online.

10. Set reasonable time limits for computer usage.

11. Check with your Internet service provider to see what parental controls they offer.

12. And if your kids ignore your warnings and have been contacted or are regularly chatting with strangers who make unusual requests (especially requests to meet in person), report it to the police for investigation.

Children with more advanced knowledge may figure out that there are ways to hide their web behaviour. For example, they may know that the history of websites visited can be deleted in web browsers (such as Google, Internet Explorer, Mozilla Firefox – programs that you used to access the Internet). So, you may never know what they were up to. Or that some applications immediately delete their chat activities. It is always important to remember to build trust with your children from an early age, so that they will come to you if they are ever requested to do something inappropriate by someone online.

How do we handle and manage bad cyber behaviour towards us?

If someone else's repeating behaviour online makes you feel uncomfortable, you may be dealing with a cyber bully. While reacting to everything you disagree with online is not a winning strategy, you have the absolute right not to be bullied online.

If someone:

- Repeatedly makes you feel uncomfortable (especially if they seem to target you and not others).

- Frequently uses humiliation, intimidation and especially threats.

It is time to take action; perhaps you can use a three-strike policy. At first, tell the person to stop (or get a friend to do so if you feel uncomfortable) as they are making you feel uncomfortable. Second, tell them (or get a friend to tell them) in no uncertain terms that what they are doing seems to fit that pattern of online bullying and if they don't stop you will be forced to take action.

If they continue to make you uncomfortable, you have every right to take measures to protect yourself,

You can:

- Report them on the forum they are using.

- Block the bully from contacting you.

- Let your friends and family know what is going on.

- Save the messages sent to you by the bully. They can be used as evidence against them.

- If necessary report them to the Internet safety authorities. In Australia, you can make a complaint to the e-safety commissioner at this website (https://www.esafety.gov.au/report/cyberbullying).

- Local police station.

- If school related, contact school or the department of education.

Team up with as many people as will join your side and expose the bully, remember bullies are cowards and fear exposure (and people who stand up to them). Do not be intimidated, you have the absolute right to stand-up for yourself and they do not have the right to harass, bully or intimidate you.

The bottom line

- Act in the online world the way you would in real life, you do not have to be an angel but nor is it wise to be a totally different person online.

- Set a good example for your children, be interested in what they are doing online if necessary nudge them away from acting in a way that is counter to their long term interests (in particular posting photos etc. online that they will come to regret).

- Is it ok to berate, insult, harass or bully someone in the real world? No it isn't, and neither is it ok online.

- If someone's (or a group of people's) repeating behaviour is making your feel uncomfortable online don't sit there and take it, team up, take action and take back control from the cyber bully and if necessary report them to the relevant authorities.

Focus 8: Cloud Security

More and more of people's information is being stored on remote servers (i.e. not on their computer's hard drive) collectively known as 'the Cloud'. These servers are owned by companies like Amazon, Google, Microsoft, Dropbox etc. and the amount of data they store is measured in Exa-bytes which is a 1 with 18 zeros (or millions of terra-bytes). So, given the enormous amount of information being placed in the Cloud, how Cloud providers (businesses we pay to use Cloud services such as Apple, Amazon) secure our information is important.

What is the Cloud?

As previously mentioned, 'the Cloud' is just a group of servers on the Internet (the Cloud is a subset of the Internet) owned by one of the big tech companies. The term 'the Cloud' is just a marketing term for their information storage/hosted computing business.

Cloud based services have always been used, whether you use Gmail or Yahoo! Mail, the email content and attachments are essentially been hosted on multiple servers on the Internet rather than on your local laptop or PC. So, your data has always been essentially stored like 'the Cloud' or the Internet somewhere...and still is.

Over the years, more and more Cloud sites, products, or services have emerged which store, process or transmit our information, this collection of Cloud sites and services is referred to as the 'Cloud network'. Technically, this network spans all over the world and your data is stored and moved around numerous countries because that is where the companies host their data centres with all their IT equipment.

The use of cloud-based storage services has also emerged, such as iCloud or Dropbox. Instead of storing your photos or documents (for example) on your computer's hard drive (which can break, be stolen or lost), you can upload your photos to a remote server owned by a tech company that promises to look after them for you and keep them safe (for a fee).

This means that you can then access your photos or document from anywhere (with Internet access) and from many different devices (think of accessing your photos or documents on your iPad, smartphone, laptop etc. from a central place). Ideally your photos/documents can be stored and retrieved as seamlessly as if these were on your computer's hard drive.

How do things operate differently in the Cloud?

It is important to understand that there are four Cloud storage scenarios:

- One is where we use services (either free or fee based), such as our email (i.e. Gmail, Yahoo! Mail etc.) that has always been hosted in the global Internet network.

- The second is where we pay to use a data-storage subscription service; recognised to be in the 'Cloud', such as Dropbox or iCloud. Here we can upload, download and work on documentation, photos, music etc. all within this one service, which is accessible via an application or website.

- The third is where we download an application (e.g. a chat application like WhatsApp) for use on our mobile phone and/or tablet where the data that we enter into that application (i.e. the chatlog) is stored in 'the Cloud network'. It is good to be aware that almost all of the applications that we use will be utilising Cloud-based services in the background; to allow the application to function properly as well as manage the users' data.

- And the fourth one is where we can purchase a bit of space (private Cloud subscriptions to virtual network services) on the Cloud network through private providers like Amazon, Google, or Azure. This type of service is more for tech savvy types, who want to set up virtual network environments and servers to operate a network for personal or business use.

Technically, the first three are what is referred to as Software as a Service model, meaning you are using a software that's hosted on the Cloud. The fourth option can be a SaaS but it can also be what's known as Platform as a Service (where the user has the flexibility to install their own software on a cloud network that provides the servers and underlying IT network) or Infrastructure as Service (where the user only pays for the IT network and has the freedom to install whatever server and software they prefer.

How should cyber security be managed in the Cloud by the Cloud provider?

Basically, in all the various scenarios described above, the essence of cyber security remains to still be:

a. Understand the data that is important to you.

b. Protect access to this data by ensuring that you choose a secure password and implement multi-factor authentication to gain access to the data; be it attachments within your email or documentation within web services such as Dropbox.

c. Limit the settings and control mechanisms that allow applications to have access to data on your tablet and mobile phone. For example, deactivate Facebook Messenger's access to your photos, try not to autosave passwords (unless there is a secure password saving application), prevent the use of Facebook/Gmail credentials to access other applications

d. Always know that when using a service or accessing a website on the Internet someone has to provide support, maintenance to that service or website. Hence, there are people with privileged access to the backend (i.e. the underlying code) of all web services and websites, who could potentially have access to your information. Maintenance and support is essential to ensure that the website or service you want to use works well for you, but it is important to be aware that someone (or more than one person) may have access to the data you are uploading there.

e. Similar principles for dealing with malware and suspicious behaviour applies in the Cloud as it does in other digital areas, that is, if you notice anything unusual in the operation of your Cloud service, stop what you are doing, take notes and screenshots of the anomaly and report it to your Cloud service customer support team.

f. Activate and use the security controls afforded by your Cloud provider, this may sound silly but many people do not use security features available to them either because they don't know to ask about them or they do not think they are important. These security features are things such as: firewall services, multi-factor authentication, logging of access attempts etc.

g. Read the terms and conditions with regard to data/information security provided by your Cloud provider and understand both your responsibilities and the Cloud provider's responsibilities with regard to protecting your data. If you have questions for them about anything in the terms and conditions, make sure they answer your questions in writing.

These are some of the areas that your Cloud provider should be on to of before you sign up with them you are entitled to ask them about their cyber security.

What happens if there is a data breach with your cloud provider?

When it comes to using the Cloud, sometimes exactly who is responsible for the security of your data is not as clear cut as you might think. If, for example, your data is illegally accessed because your login credentials were stolen from your side (i.e. you shared it, wrote it down, left access open) or you used a weak password, then the responsibility for the security breach is with you.

If there is a large-scale compromise of your Cloud provider (i.e. thousands of accounts are hacked) it is the provider's responsibility because it is likely that the hack is of a much more sophisticated nature and it the provider's responsibility for repelling attacks by cyber crooks that the average person cannot be expected to handle (i.e. those beyond the scope of this guide for example). In these instances, it is also the provider's responsibility to notify you of the security breach so you can change your passwords and check data has not been lost etc. (Note: in Australia now, this is a legal requirement via the Data Breach Notification law whereby if your day hosted by a company was stolen or breached, you need to be notified). This is the way responsibilities should be divided by it is worth confirming this with your Cloud provider before you sign-up.

The bottom line

- You have a right to grill your Cloud service provider on what information security they provide to you. I.e. how they will secure your data and what will happen in the event of a breach.

- As with previous areas of information security, if something seems off about your data or how it is stored, take action; call your Cloud provider and ask them questions and if you don't like the answer consider going elsewhere for Cloud services.

- Consider the information you are storing on the Cloud, if worst comes to worst, can you afford for it to be stolen or transmitted without your knowledge (no Cloud security is infallible) if the answer is no, consider alternative methods of storage for this information.

- Know that access to you Cloud can occur through your credentials, so how you manage it securely is your responsibility. This means constantly changing your password, using multi-factor authentication, not sharing your login or leaving yourself logged in etc.

Focus 9: Home Network Security

We mostly understand a home networks to consist of multiple devices connected via a wireless network (technically referred to as a Home Local Area Network). This usually consists of a central device, a wireless modem/router, which is connected to an Internet access point via a cable (set up by your Internet Service Provider) giving you access to the Internet network (technically referred to as a Wide Area Network (WAN). The devices (i.e. laptop, smart phone, and tablet) are connected via single-sign-in (SSI) and a password (your wireless router password) and access the Internet via radio transmissions (i.e. Wi-Fi signals).

Your wireless router is the gateway to accessing the Internet from your home and it is via compromising this router that crooks can get access to devices connected to it and use this access to launch further attempts to steal your data such as: man-in-the-middle attacks or eavesdropping, meaning 'listening' for sensitive information that they can use to gain some advantage over you.

It's important to note here that you can access the Internet by plugging a cable (technically referred to as a network cable) from the wireless router to your laptop or device, rather than accessing the Internet via a Wi-Fi signal. This is a more secure approach because the data is transferred via a wire (which can only be attacked by accessing it physically similar to old style 'phone tapping') whereas accessing wireless communication between your device and the Wi-Fi signal (using your devices Wi-Fi card) can be done by a cyber crook parked outside your house 'listening' to communication on your wireless network.

What is a home network?

As previously stated, a home network tends to consist of multiple devices connected to a wireless router, that is, the devices connected to a wireless router comprise your home network. More and more devices in homes are now connected via a home network – laptops, mobile phones, printers, television, the fridge, baby monitors etc. the trend seems to be an ever-increasing list of devices being added to your home network. The collection of all devices or appliances connected to the Internet has been given the label 'the Internet of Things (IoT)' where formally separate devices can now talk to each other via the Internet or your home network.

An example of a home wireless network:

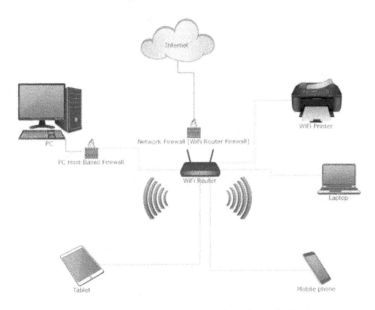

Home Network, many devices connected to central wireless router to access the Internet.

The downside to this connectivity is that malware can now propagate through a network of connected devices, whereas before unconnected devices were impervious to malware/ viruses from other unconnected devices etc. That is, before, your phone could not transmit a virus to your laptop but if they are connected in a home network, this is now a possibility. And hackers can get access to one device via the other connected devices. It is for this reason that a strong digital door is required for a home network.

You may think that this is unlikely to happen or why would they target you. In the past, everyday people (i.e. not businesses) have been targeted through emails (such as phishing) for monetary gains. It was mostly to get access to banking or credit card information to commit fraud and this is still the big motivator, but some people will hack your home network for fun, just to see if they can do it. These hacks range from just annoying to potentially harmful for you, try searching for 'baby monitor hacks' and read some real-life stories about what hackers are capable of. It is better that these annoying people meet a strong digital door. After all they have no business interfering in your home network.

Initial steps you can take to make your home network more secure:

Note that your user manual of your devices will explain how to do these things, if you get stuck, a simple Internet search will provide you more detailed explanations.

1. Change the Service Set Identifier (SSID), aka your default wireless network name so it is difficult to determine the wireless router type, that is, if your wireless router is called Linksys model 3 etc and you change the SSID to 'Fred's home network' it makes it harder for a cyber crook to find your router's vulnerability (your user manual will explain how you can do this). If the manufacturer, model and type of your wireless router becomes known, its weaknesses or vulnerabilities are easy to guess. Do not also name it in such a way to reveal too much personal info.

2. Set a strong and unique wireless network password; change the default password (see chapter 2 on choosing passwords) because a lot of the time your default password will be extremely weak i.e.

'password' or 'admin'. And if the wireless router model is known, crooks can track down the user manual which might contain the default password, or it might be on a sticker on similar models. So do not keep the pre-set default username and password, which is needed to install and connect the router, change it as soon as your wireless router is set up.

3. Set a strong network administrator password for access to your wireless router admin section i.e. settings etc (see chapter 2 on password security). Most of the time, the default username and password tend to me 'admin' or 'password'.

4. Activate Wi-Fi encryption. Note good Wi-Fi encryption is considered a hard target by cyber crooks they would much rather attack your router which has more vulnerabilities than attempt to decrypt data that the router sends to your devices.

There are three options:

a. WPA - Wi-Fi Protected Access. The algorithm used in this has been previously compromised so crooks can find a way to easily learn the method to break this.

b. WEP - Wired Equivalent Privacy: This option is extremely easy to crack and is considered by cyber crooks as an open invitation to compromise your data. The algorithm used in this has been previously compromised so crooks can find a way to easily learn the method to break this.

    c.   WPA2 - Wi-Fi Protected Access 2 is the current standard. This is the current recommended and more secure than the above 2 there is also:

        i.   WPA2 AES - Wi-Fi Protected Access 2 Advanced Encryption Standard (AES) a more advanced version of WPA2.

        ii. WPA3 - Wi-Fi Protected Access 3 is on its way as of 2020.

5.   Turn off or disable your wireless router and any connected devices when not in use or if you are away for long length of time, if the devices or the router is not powered on, they are not vulnerable to attack.

6.   Put your wireless router in the middle of your house if possible so your wireless network doesn't extend too far beyond your house. A wireless network operating in the 2.4 GHz band (most home wireless routers) will extend about 15 m inside (depending on obstacles in the house) and about 30 m outside your house if placed near an external wall.

7.   Disable remote access to your wireless router: this should be done by default, but it is still good to check as sometimes it is enabled after you seek tech support from your Internet service provider. Remote access enables you to connect to your wireless router from anywhere in the world via the World Wide Web, instead of only if you are connected to it via your home network, that is, remote access doesn't require you to enter your wireless password to get access to your wireless router interface. Disable this

feature if it is enabled as you don't generally need remote access to your wireless router, but it is very handy for a cyber crook.

8. Change the default wireless router IP address (which is usually http://192.168.1.1 or 192.168.0.1) to stop a cyber crook easily guessing it. Note this is a more extreme measure.

9. Turn off the Dynamic Host Configuration Protocol (DHCP) server in your router and use static IP addresses that you assign manually for devices that you want to connect to your home network. DHCP is the functionality in your wireless router that automatically assigns devices on your home network their IP address (address on your network). So if your router's IP address is 192.168.0.1, it will assign your phone 192.168.0.2 and your laptop 192.168.0.3 etc.

   The reason you turn off DHCP is so that your wireless router doesn't automatically assign all new devices (i.e. including a cyber crooks laptop) an IP address to connect to your wireless network. Note this step is much more effective if you change the default IP address of your wireless router as described in step 8. Both step 8 and 9 are more extreme security measures.

10. Similarly, do the applicable steps above i.e. 1-9 on any devices that you connect to your wireless network. Most of the time, the model name and password for your connected devices (i.e. laptop and phone) can be found on the Internet on public ally published admin guides or support material.

If someone identifies a way to crack into these devices (i.e. a cleaver little hacker finds vulnerabilities in the code used to design these devices) it is usually published on the Internet, so the chance of getting compromised is real. So for WiFi connected baby monitors, TVs, walkie talkies, toys etc.... change the default device name and passwords, and do not connect them the Internet if you don't need to!

How to make your home network more secure on an ongoing basis:

After you have taken the initial steps outlined above to secure your network, your next step is to install/enable firewall(s) on your wireless router and devices.

The purpose of a firewall is to protect whatever is behind the firewall from malicious network traffic (i.e. data or commands). A firewall acts like a road block manned by police on a digital highway stopping malicious data packets (i.e. Internet data or commands) in their tracks according to a list of security rules, which can either be a default list or a bespoke list of rules designed to stop specific threats.

If a firewall is installed/activated on your wireless router it is known as a network firewall as it is a barrier between networks (i.e. the Internet and your home network). A network firewall will protect every device downstream of it or behind the router (i.e. your PC, smartphone, iPad etc). If a firewall is installed on your PC (called a host-based firewall) it will only protect your PC from malicious Internet traffic.

Note that Windows has had an inbuilt host-based firewall since Windows XP whereas Mac OS X has a firewall but it must be activated by the user. Alternatively, you can purchase firewall software if you feel that there are better options out there than the default firewall on your device.

Many people are unaware their wireless router comes with a network-based firewall, check if your wireless router has a firewall by logging into your admin page and if it has a firewall, enable it if it currently disabled.

Tip: To log into your wireless router's admin functionality open up a browser window and type in your router's IP address ; it will be something like 192.168.1.1, unless you have changed it, consult your wireless router user manual for the correct address.

The bottom line

- Secure your wireless router with a strong password, encryption.

- Make sure your wireless router has a firewall and that it is enabled it if it is currently disabled. If your wireless router does not have a firewall, consider buying another wireless router that does have one.

- Secure your devices with host-based firewalls, as well as antivirus (or endpoint security solutions).

- Do not connect devices to your home wireless network if you don't need to.

- ALWAYS change default passwords on devices.

Focus 10: Physical Security

It is all very well to secure your digital devices using digital means but that is not much use to you if your digital device gets stolen the old fashion way e.g. via a rock through your back window. While it is beyond the scope of this guide to provide detailed information on physical home security, there are some simple measures you can take to prevent your digital device from walking out your physical front door.

How can access be obtained to my property?

Once you know what forms your property to protect, it's good to think about how people could access this property, not just by the front or back door, which are the obvious. But think about other openings, how many entry and exit points are there and how are these controlled, for example:

- Are there ground floor windows and how are these locked?

- Are there other windows that someone can climb, open and access into your property?

- Are there entry points on your roof? Or accessible opening to underground part of your property?

- How many adjacent buildings are there? Are these well protected or can someone come from that property to yours?

- Are there cars parked nearby to the building or perimeter? Can anyone park there or do they need a valid parking permit?

- Is there easy access to telecommunication lines or meters, and can this be used to cause harm to you?

- How well are all the access paths lightening controlled?

How is access to your property protected?

There are common methods to try stop people who want to gain access to your property and most of these you already probably use or of which you are aware.

If you are using locks and keys like most people, how you store and secure these keys when they are not in use is probably the most important step. For example, someone could take your keys when you are out and about, or from within your house without you knowing. So, if this happens, immediately change your locks. You could consider using combination locks rather than lock and key for added security.

In addition to your front door, it is also important to secure the things in your house which are very important to you. If you choose to use combination locks, make sure that you do not share the numbers with anyone else and change the numbers every so often. (E.g. if your friend or partner move on from living with you and they previously knew your combination).

How is unpermitted access detected?

In addition to trying to stop people getting into your property, if you think it is worthwhile, implementing a method to detect whether someone is trying to get in could also be a good idea.

The standard method by which we do this is to use an alarm. It is up to you to decide whether you want to secure the entire property or a specific part (i.e. all windows and external doors) with alarm? And if you want to manage that alarm yourself or link it to a service, inclusive of notifying the police when it is activated. It is important to not just have an alarm but a plan on what should be done and by whom when and if the alarm does go off due to intruders.

More and more homes are using CCTV to record activities that are occurring around their property, especially in the hours when they are asleep because this is when perpetrators tend to check out ways to try get access. If this is something that you want to install, consider whether you want to just monitor the outside (external) environment or parts of inside (internal) environment. Alarms to be linked to the CCTV, and the CCTV footage can work in low light and record the events. It's important to also think about recording the footage and how long will you want to keep it archived. If what you are trying to protect is so valuable, you may want someone (like a security guard) to always monitor the footage live or just film and keep it recorded.

Some simple tips on home security

There are many other things you can do to make your home more secure but like cyber security, physical security is all about making yourself a hard target (not invulnerable) so that a thief will move on and look for something a bit easier. In short physical security is about deterrence as much as anything else. The following is a list of steps you can take to make your property and therefore your information and data stored in your property too hard a target for a thief to bother with.

- Make sure your door is secure and cannot be easily kicked in (a common way to break into a house), think about adding a security door.

- Add automatic lighting to your front porch this is handy for your but will also deter house thieves who prefer to operate in the dark.

- Make sure your windows lock (including windows on the second story).

- Install an alarm (or at least put an alarm company sticker on your house).

- Put a 'beware of the dog' sticker on your side gate (even if you do not have a dog).

- Do not leave things lying around your house that will assist a thief to break in (i.e. a ladder, or hammer).

- Do not announce on social media when you are going away on a long holiday and where you will be staying, and for how long.

- If you do go away make sure a friend or family member comes passed you house every so often to collect the mail, an overflowing letterbox is a good sign for a thief that no one is home.

- Do not leave what is inside your house visible from the outside, thieves call this window shopping, cover your windows with blinds (especially when you are not at home).

- Don't leave you digital devices lying around if you go out or away on a trip, hide them or lock them away, thieves want to get out of your house as soon as possible and will tend to grab what is easily accessible i.e. your TV or anything of value lying around.

The bottom line

- Review your home security from the point of view of a thief are you an easy target for a break in? If you are implementing the suggestions from the list above and make yourself a hard target.

- Compare your level of security to other people in your neighbourhood are you the weakest link, if you are you need to at least match the security level of your neighbours to avoid being the obvious target for a thief.

In Conclusion

We have looked at the ten main areas of focus for cyber security, from deciding what data is important to you and choosing a strong password to the basics of beefing up your home network security. Having read this guide, you now have more knowledge about how to secure you digital door than the vast majority of computer users out there. You might not be a cyber security expert but you have enough information to make yourself a hard target, tough enough to deter the average cyber crook into looking for an easier mark.

As you implement the recommendations in this guide and grow in your understanding of how to take cyber security in your own hands, don't forget to pass this information on to others so that every door in your digital neighbourhood is as strong as yours will be.

GLOSSARY OF TERMS

Apps: Short for applications a fancy name for a computer program that does something useful.

ACSC: Australian Cyber Security Centre, the national organisation for cyber security in Australia

Admin: Short for administrator, the highest level of privileged access to a particular program usually distinguished by the ability to delete or modify files.

The Cloud: A group of servers on the Internet managed by a tech company that are used by people either free or for a fee to store data.

The Clearweb: The part of the Internet that can be readily accessed using common search engines like Yahoo! and Google.

DHCP: Dynamic Host Configuration Protocol the functionality that automatically assigns devices an IP address on your wireless network.

Dropbox: A service that allows you to store a limited amount of data online for free with a fee payable for larger amounts of data.

Darkweb: The part of the Internet only accessible using specialist software like a Tor browser where browsers are usually anonymous. Not exclusively used by criminals but a lot of criminal activity occurs here.

Deepweb: The part of the Internet that is not readily accessible by normal search engines and comprises 95% + of the Internet i.e. data behind paywalls, in the Cloud or not index by search engines etc.

Host- based firewall: A software-based firewall to prevent malicious data packets implemented at the device level i.e. on your laptop.

IoT: The Internet of Things, a fancy name for devices in the home that are connected to your home wireless network and thus the Internet

IP address: Internet Protocol address, equivalent to your devices' home address on the Internet.

Man in the middle: where the cyber crook relays or possibly alters communication between two parties making them believe they are communicating directly with each other. The aim is to either eaves drop on communication or to deliver false messages to either party with to gain some advantage over them.

Malware: or malicious software; includes viruses but also all software that is intended to do harm to a user.

Multifactor Security: Another level of security beyond your username and password e.g. a code sent to your mobile to log on to a service or complete a transaction.

Network firewall: A firewall (hardware based i.e. on your wireless router) that operates as a barrier between networks i.e. your home network and the Internet.

NIST: the Nation Institute of Standards and Technology is the American body that sets technology standards.

OS: Operating system i.e. MacOS, Windows 7, Windows 10 etc.

PC: Personal computer

Phishing: a specific type of scam that gets you to upload data to a fake website (often designed to look legitimate) that is sent to you as a link in an email with a convincing story as to why you should click on it.

USB: Universal Serial Bus also used to refer to flash drives i.e. small easily portable solid state drives that store data.

User: the person using the computer or program, this title is usually given to the lowest level of privileged access to a program or service and usually does not have rights to modify or delete data.

RSA SecurID: Either a physical object or software that creates a unique code assigned to you every 60 seconds, for example. This code must be entered in the time period it exists along with your username and password if you want to gain access to your data.

Scam watch: an Australian government website where people can report online scams.

SSI: Single Sign In, where a single sign in barrier allows you access to multiple related systems

SSID: Service Set Identifier also known as your home network's name.

SSL: Secure Socket Layer, a security standard for establishing an encrypted Internet connection.

VPN: Virtual Private Network, software that encrypts your traffic between your computer and a server (often in a different country), the result being your computer's IP address is hidden and therefore cannot be traced or attacked.